PRINCETON STUDIES IN INTERNATIONAL FINANCE

No. 85, June 1999

TRANSITION STRATEGIES: CHOICES AND OUTCOMES

HOLGER C. WOLF

INTERNATIONAL FINANCE SECTION

DEPARTMENT OF ECONOMICS
PRINCETON UNIVERSITY
PRINCETON, NEW JERSEY

Library of Congress Cataloging-in-Publication Data

Wolf, Holger C.
Transition strategies : choices and outcomes / Holger C. Wolf.
p. cm. — (Princeton studies in international finance, ISSN 0081-8070 ; no. 85)
Includes bibliographical references.
ISBN 0-88165-257-1 (pbk.)
1. Europe, Eastern—Economic policy—1989- 2. Europe, Eastern—Economic conditions—1989- 3. Former Soviet republics—Economic policy. 4. Former Soviet republics—Economic conditions. 5. Postcommunism—Economic aspects. I. Title. II. Series.
HC244.W65 1999
338.947—dc21 99-13184
CIP

Printed in the United States of America by Princeton University Printing Services at Princeton, New Jersey

International Standard Serial Number: 0081-8070
International Standard Book Number: 0-88165-257-1
Library of Congress Catalog Card Number: 99-13184

CONTENTS

TABLES

1 INTRODUCTION

The transition from planned to market economies in Central and Eastern Europe has been traumatic. The Schumpeterian process unleashed as economies rushed toward market systems was initially destructive. Production levels collapsed while inflation surged, ravaging the savings of the middle classes and eroding the living standards of large segments of the population (Atkinson and Micklewright, 1992). A few years into the transition, the expected "blooming landscapes" remained *fata morganas*, apart from a few bright spots in the Visigrad countries.

The second half of the 1990s has improved the picture substantially. Among the leading reformers, Poland seems to be firmly on track toward establishing a pluralistic market economy. It can expect European Union (EU) membership in the not too distant future. The other Visigrad countries are not far behind. A second group of EU applicants—Bulgaria, Latvia, Lithuania, Romania, and the Slovak Republic—have made substantial progress, as have a few of the Soviet successor states, notably the Kyrgyz Republic and Moldova.

Yet, the success of the transition lags behind early expectations. The change from pervasive state control to pluralistic societies and adequately functioning market economies remains partial; indeed, several transition economies have recently regressed. On many measures, material living standards for large subsections of the population, notably the socially weakest groups, have so significantly declined that the specter of Weimar has become a popular benchmark. This has occurred even as opportunities and choices for the better qualified and younger population groups have expanded. The aggregate payoff to reform has been less than expected, at least using official statistics. According to estimates of the European Bank for Reconstruction and Development (EBRD), the average 1998 real gross domestic product (GDP) for the region was 72 percent of that for the pretransition level, with only three

I am grateful for helpful comments received from Samuel Barnes, Helge Berger, John Cuddington, Robert Cumby, Anne-Marie Gulde, Cevdet Denizer, Harmen Lehment, Monika Schnitzer, Horst Siebert, and seminar participants at Georgetown University, Princeton University, the Kiel Institute of World Economics, and the University of Munich.

transition economies recording output above the 1989 level, and these three by only small margins.[1] Far from experiencing rapid catch-up over the last decade, the transition economies have thus fallen farther behind the EU, a development that has come largely as a surprise to both eastern and western observers.[2]

Almost ten years after the initial reforms, the challenge of transition is rapidly being replaced by the more generic challenge of development. The end of this early phase provides an opportunity to draw lessons from the varied experiences of the transition economies. Indeed, the transition period provides a rare natural experiment in comparative economics. Twenty-five countries began the transition from planned to market economies at roughly the same time, but they started from different initial conditions, followed different strategies, and moved at different speeds. Their comparative experiences thus provide a unique opportunity to study the interactions among starting points, political economy, and reform choices and outcomes.

[1] The three are Poland (118), the Slovak Republic (100), and Slovenia (103), with 1989 equaling 100. The problems in comparing pre- and posttransition output levels from a welfare perspective are, of course, well known.

[2] Witness, *inter alia*, the Shatalin program envisaging completion of the transition within 500 days. Ironically, Lenin estimated that the time necessary for the transition from a market to a socialist economy would be 100 years.

2 TRANSITION STRATEGIES

A chasm cannot be crossed in two steps.

—Vaclav Klaus

The wise man tests the stones before crossing the river.

—Chinese proverb

The sudden collapse of socialism in Central and Eastern Europe in the years after 1989 caught economists largely off guard. Although libraries could be filled with books detailing the "inevitable" move from capitalism to socialism, very few studies had examined the mechanics of the opposite transition, the reestablishment of markets in centrally planned economies.

In the face of political collapse, pressing decisions could not be delayed to await the outcome of scientific debate. Early proposals for transition strategies rapidly coalesced around two poles. One school of thought viewed the transition as a magnified example of the structural-adjustment problems encountered elsewhere in distorted market economies. In consequence, the multi-ingredient remedies applied to those economies—rapid and comprehensive liberalization of prices and trade; current-account convertibility often coupled with the introduction of a pegged exchange rate; conservative fiscal and monetary policies; and comprehensive removal of market distortions—was expected also to cure the transition malaise.

Labeled variously as the "big bang," "cold turkey," or "radical" approach to transition, this view dominated the early debate and retains strong support, particularly in the Anglo-Saxon academic and policy circles. A flavor of this view is given by David Lipton and Jeffrey Sachs (1990, p. 99), both closely involved in the Polish reform. Writing very early in the transition process, they assert that "both the economic logic and the political situation argue for a rapid and comprehensive process of transition. History . . . has taught the profound shortcomings of a piecemeal approach, and economic logic suggests the feasibility of a rapid transition." Similar views were held by some of the early reformers in Central Europe; see, for example, Vaclav Klaus's (1993) "Ten Commandments," as well as Klaus (1991) and Balcerowicz and Gelb (1994).

Apart from economic arguments, based explicitly or implicitly on the theory of second best, proponents of rapid reform also pointed to political-economy advantages of moving early and comprehensively to dismantle the old system and exploit "windows of opportunity" to establish new ground rules that would lend credibility while tying the hands of future governments. As one of the key architects of the Polish reform notes, "radical economic reform creates safeguards to make the transition process irreversible. It rapidly introduces a number of economic and institutional changes that act as policy constraints on any new government taking over, whatever their basic ideology and value system" (Balcerowicz, 1993, p. 2).

The second school of thought questions the interpretation of the transition as a magnified problem in structural adjustment and reform. It argues that the nearly complete absence of both markets and market-supporting institutions renders inapplicable the key advantage of the orthodox approach, the reaping of instant efficiency gains by removing the fetters from existing, but suppressed, markets. In the absence of institutions that can effectively transmit scarcity signals, and set incentives to react to such signals, the neoclassical prescription is held to be inappropriate. The transition is viewed as a distinct problem in search of a distinct solution, requiring greater emphasis on "microeconomic reforms over the macroeconomic focus of many of the original Anglo-Saxon reform blueprints" (Siebert, Raiser, and Langhammer, 1996, p. 8). Somewhat ironically, the case for gradualism also derives its intellectual support from second-best theory. Whereas proponents of radical reform argue that the potential gains from reforms are limited by stepwise liberalization, such as the removing of price controls without dismantling the market power of existing monopolies through trade liberalization, proponents of gradual reform emphasize the need to distinguish between legal and effective reform and to understand that the latter will take time. Thus, following price liberalization, the legal abolition of restrictions on the entry of new firms may be insufficient to avoid monopoly pricing by incumbents if entry of new domestic and foreign competitors fails to occur owing to a lack of supporting institutions such as accessible distribution networks, access to bank credit, effective regulation, and legal protections. In like vein, the imposition of hard budget constraints on enterprises in the absence of functioning credit may force even sound firms into insolvency. Liberalization in the absence of supporting institutions can, in consequence, deepen the "transformational recession" unnecessarily (Dewatripont and Roland, 1992; Kornai, 1992, 1994; Laban and Wolf, 1993;

Murrell, 1993, 1995, 1996; Amsden, Kochanowicz, and Taylor, 1994; Taylor, 1994).

By stressing the difference, and the time lag, between the legal removal of obstacles and the effective emergence of the previously impeded institutions, gradual transition strategies tend to emphasize the active and necessarily time-consuming process of nurturing institutions and market infrastructure as a crucial condition for, and constraint on the timing of, successful liberalization. "Economic reforms in transition economies should start with the build-up of an institutional infrastructure before prices are liberalized" (Siebert, Raiser, and Langhammer, 1996, p. 8).[1]

Beyond these differences, radical and gradual transition recipes share many common elements. Yet it is fair to say that policymakers in the early transition economies were faced with a wide disparity of external and internal advice, without having much empirical basis to judge alternatives. The variety of strategies actually adopted matches the variety of the recommendations received. One group of transition economies—notably the Czech Republic, Estonia, and Poland—by and large embraced the radical-transition recipe. Near-simultaneous stabilization and liberalization was followed by rapid privatization. The private-sector share of GDP—perhaps the single best indicator of progress in the transition from planned to market economies has reached 80 percent in Hungary and 75 percent in Albania and the Czech and Slovak Republics, above the level of several countries in the Organisation for Economic Co-operation and Development (OECD).

A second group of countries, comprising Bulgaria, Moldova, and Romania, has more closely followed the gradual path, showing slow but reasonably steady liberalization (occasional reversals notwithstanding) and reaching private shares of GDP of between 45 and 60 percent. Others, however, including Belarus, Tajikistan, and Uzbekistan, have barely commenced the transition. Seven years after the collapse of the Soviet Union, the private-sector share of GDP remains at 20 percent in Belarus, 30 percent in Tajikistan, and 25 percent in Turkmenistan.

[1] See Balcerowicz (1993, 1995, 1997), Sachs (1993), Weitzman (1993), Aghion and Blanchard (1994), Aslund (1994), and Balcerowicz and Gelb (1994) for alternative views of the political economy of transition. The cited works on the radical approach are from the early transition period. Over time, the "Cambridge Consensus," including the cited authors, has placed increasing emphasis on social-protection measures. In this sense at least, the two approaches have increasingly converged.

3 DATA

The data set used to explore the nexus between strategy choice, initial conditions, and outcomes includes the twenty-five East European transition countries for which comparable performance data and indicators of policy choice are available for the period from 1989 to 1995. These are the fifteen successor countries of the former Soviet Union (FSU)—Armenia, Azerbaijan, Belarus, Estonia, Georgia, Kazakhstan, the Kyrgyz Republic, Latvia, Lithuania, Moldova, Russia, Tajikistan, Turkmenistan, Ukraine, Uzbekistan—and most of the Central and South European transition countries—Albania, Bulgaria, Croatia, the Czech Republic, Hungary, FYR Macedonia, Poland, Romania, Slovakia, and Slovenia. The transition economies of Asia and Africa are excluded because a matching data set could not be obtained for them. Although their exclusion is unfortunate from the viewpoint of completeness, it increases the homogeneity of the data set, which eases the task of identifying the impact of differences in choices of transition strategies (Sachs, 1996).

Because the statistical agencies of the transition countries were initially ill equipped to handle the data demands of a market economy, data availability and quality is spotty in the early years.[1] The database underlying this study was therefore constructed from a wide variety of sources, including country reports from the International Monetary Fund (IMF), the World Bank, the Economist Intelligence Unit, and PlanEcon; the World Bank's 1995 *World Development Report* (1996); the EBRD's *Transition Report* (1994, 1995); the U.S. Central Intelligence Agency's *World Factbook*; the IMF's *World Economic Outlook*, *International Financial Statistics*, and databases; government financial statistics, and a number of scholarly articles.

To avoid outlier bias, all nominal growth observations—broad money growth, nominal-income growth, growth of the consumer price index

[1] The World Bank (1993) provides an extensive discussion of data issues. See also Lipton and Sachs (1990), Winiecki (1991), Aslund (1994), Koen (1994), and Bloem, Cotterell, and Gigantes (1996). These data problems are particularly acute in interpreting output changes over time from a welfare perspective (Berg and Sachs, 1992). Although serious, however, they are arguably less severe for comparisons across transition economies suffering from similar mismeasurements.

(CPI), and the GDP deflator—have been rescaled as $x/(1 + x)$, where x is the unscaled observation. The transformation leaves small growth rates substantially unchanged but compresses large growth rates, reducing the importance of hyperinflation observations in the regressions.

The indicator of transition-strategy choice is the aggregate annual reform index constructed by de Melo, Denizer, and Gelb (1996; updated), based on a consistent survey of World Bank country economists. The index covers three broad areas: (1) the extent of regulations on external trade, including quantity and convertibility restrictions, (2) restrictions on the creation of new firms, and (3) restrictions on prices. The aggregate index reported by de Melo, Denizer, and Gelb is based on an average of these three subindices and ranges between 0 and 1, with 1 defined as a degree of liberalization comparable to the average OECD economy. Table 1 reports the index values.

Although most of the regressions are based on this continuous measure, it is instructive to begin with a derived discrete grouping of transition economies into *radical*, *gradual*, and *lagging* reformers. Using such a grouping provides a more direct way of assessing initial conditions and performance under alternative regimes, albeit at the cost of introducing additional subjectivity (see Table 2).

- A country is defined as *radical* reformer if its liberalization index has jumped by at least 0.4 over any two-year period and equals at least 0.7 at the end of the sample, that is, if a country has fairly rapidly moved fairly close to full liberalization. The definitions as well as the classification, are, of course, subjective. The radical rating applies to the year in which the jump is completed and to all subsequent years.

- A country is defined as a *gradual* reformer if it breaches the 0.7 threshold in the final sample year but does not undertake a sufficiently rapid liberalization to generate a 0.4 jump over any two-year period in its index. In addition, the prejump years of the radical reformers fall into this group.

- Finally, a country is defined as a *lagging* reformer if its terminal liberalization index is below 0.7.

The inclusion of the laggard group allows for a distinction between countries such as Slovenia, which is pursuing a full liberalization at a deliberately slow pace, and countries such as Belarus, which is not pursuing liberalization. It thus avoids creating a potential bias in favor of radical reformers, generated by commingling gradual reformers with laggards. On the downside, restricting the label of "gradual reformers" to countries that achieve a high degree of liberalization at the end of

TABLE 1

LIBERALIZATION INDEX, 1989–1995

	1989	1990	1991	1992	1993	1994	1995
Successor states of the FSU							
Armenia	0.04	0.04	0.13	0.39	0.42	0.42	0.58
Azerbaijan	0.04	0.04	0.04	0.25	0.31	0.35	0.44
Belarus	0.04	0.04	0.10	0.20	0.33	0.36	0.48
Estonia	0.07	0.20	0.32	0.64	0.81	0.89	0.93
Georgia	0.04	0.04	0.22	0.32	0.35	0.35	0.49
Kazakhstan	0.04	0.04	0.14	0.35	0.35	0.39	0.57
Kyrgyz Republic	0.04	0.04	0.04	0.33	0.60	0.76	0.82
Latvia	0.04	0.13	0.29	0.51	0.67	0.81	0.81
Lithuania	0.04	0.13	0.33	0.55	0.75	0.89	0.86
Moldova	0.04	0.04	0.10	0.38	0.51	0.55	0.68
Russia	0.04	0.04	0.10	0.49	0.59	0.66	0.69
Tajikistan	0.04	0.04	0.11	0.20	0.26	0.30	0.39
Turkmenistan	0.04	0.04	0.04	0.13	0.16	0.22	0.22
Ukraine	0.04	0.04	0.10	0.23	0.13	0.26	0.51
Uzbekistan	0.04	0.04	0.04	0.26	0.30	0.43	0.53
Central and South European transition economies							
Albania	0.00	0.00	0.24	0.66	0.70	0.70	0.74
Bulgaria	0.13	0.19	0.62	0.66	0.66	0.64	0.61
Croatia	0.41	0.62	0.62	0.72	0.79	0.82	0.85
Czech Republic	0.00	0.16	0.79	0.86	0.90	0.90	0.93
FYR Macedonia	0.41	0.62	0.65	0.68	0.78	0.78	0.78
Hungary	0.34	0.57	0.74	0.78	0.82	0.86	0.90
Poland	0.24	0.68	0.72	0.82	0.82	0.86	0.89
Romania	0.00	0.22	0.36	0.45	0.58	0.68	0.71
Slovakia	0.00	0.16	0.79	0.86	0.86	0.86	0.86
Slovenia	0.41	0.62	0.71	0.78	0.82	0.82	0.85

SOURCE: De Melo, Denizer, and Gelb (1996)

the sample misclassifies countries that initially pursue a gradual strategy but fail to fully implement it throughout the sample period.

By depending on the terminal value of the liberalization index, this definition employs hindsight: three countries having the same liberalization value in 1990 might be variously classified as having been radical, gradual, and lagging in 1990, depending on their policy choices from 1991 to 1995. This could, in some cases, give rise to classifications differing from those that informed observers would have chosen at the time and that might, therefore, have been the bases for investment and consumption choices. To allow for this possibility, the robustness of the

TABLE 2

STRATEGY CLASSIFICATION, 1989–1995

	1989	1990	1991	1992	1993	1994	1995
Successor states of the FSU							
Armenia	L	L	L	L	L	L	L
Azerbaijan	L	L	L	L	L	L	L
Belarus	L	L	L	L	L	L	L
Estonia	G	G	G	R	R	R	R
Georgia	L	L	L	L	L	L	L
Kazakhstan	L	L	L	L	L	L	L
Kyrgyz Republic	G	G	G	G	R	R	R
Latvia	G	G	G	G	G	G	G
Lithuania	G	G	G	R	R	R	R
Moldova	L	L	L	L	L	L	L
Russia	L	L	L	L	L	L	L
Tajikistan	L	L	L	L	L	L	L
Turkmenistan	L	L	L	L	L	L	L
Ukraine	L	L	L	L	L	L	L
Uzbekistan	L	L	L	L	L	L	L
Central and South European transition economies							
Albania	G	G	G	R	R	R	R
Bulgaria	L	L	L	L	L	L	L
Croatia	G	G	G	G	G	G	G
Czech Republic	G	G	R	R	R	R	R
FYR Macedonia	G	G	G	G	G	G	G
Hungary	G	G	R	R	R	R	R
Poland	G	G	R	R	R	R	R
Romania	G	G	G	G	G	G	G
Slovakia	G	G	R	R	R	R	R
Slovenia	G	G	G	G	G	G	G

NOTE: R = radical reformer; G = gradual reformer; L = lagging reformer.

results were tested by also using an alternative classification including only contemporaneous information.

Under this alternative index, a country is defined as radical if the liberalization index has increased by at least 0.4 over the current or a previous two-year period and equals at least 0.7. If the index equals or exceeds 0.7 but has not shown a 0.4 point jump in any prior two-year period, the country is classified as gradual. The residual observations are defined as laggard. The main difference between the two schemes is the classification of the early observations for countries ultimately breaching the 0.7 threshold. These are rated as gradual under the first scheme but as laggard under the second. The second classification captures changes in the transition strategy that occur during the sample period, but it fails in the initial years to capture the difference between a country pursuing deliberately gradual reform and a country pursuing no reform at all. In practice, the two classifications give quite similar results for medians, the preferred statistic. To keep the discussion at a manageable length, I report results for only the first classification.

4 THE OUTCOME: A FIRST LOOK

Much as the transition itself was largely unexpected, its economic virulence has come as a surprise to most observers. Although an output decline of some magnitude was expected as economically inefficient firms closed down, the magnitude of the decline dwarfed most initial predictions. Table 3 provides a first look at the growth performance of the transition economies, reporting the median, maximum, and minimum growth rates for the twenty-five transition economies examined in this study.

TABLE 3

GDP GROWTH RATES

	1989	1990	1991	1992	1993	1994	1995	1996	1997
Median	1.5	-3.5	-11.7	-13.6	-10.0	0.3	0.8	3.0	4.0
Maximum	9.8	9.0	-1.0	2.6	9.6	9.4	7.8	10.5	10.0
Minimum	-7.2	-12.0	-28.0	-52.4	-39.0	-35.0	-17.4	-10.0	-4.0

SOURCES: IMF, EBRD, PlanEcon, World Bank.

Real output growth has followed a J-curve, with a sharp decline in the initial years followed by a rebound more recently. The initial decline was shared to a large degree across the transition economies: a simple regression of output growth rates on time dummies for Central Europe and the FSU explains 56 percent of the variance of the growth rates. The similarity of output movements suggests the importance of the effect of common exogenous shocks on the transition economies, including the disruption of established domestic lines of decision-making, the breakdown of the external trading system, the deterioration in the payments system, and the severe deterioration in the terms of trade for energy importers.

Table 4 reports the median, maximum, and minimum for the CPI inflation rate, revealing an initial inflation burst followed by stabilization in some, though by no means all, transition economies. Shared factors again played an important role, particularly early in the transition, as inherited excess real balances were eroded through inflation and as the non-oil-producing transition economies experienced significant increases in the price of energy imports.

TABLE 4

CPI INFLATION RATES

	1989	1990	1991	1992	1993	1994	1995	1996	1997
Median	4.6	13.9	97.8	865.3	921.0	139.1	43.0	19.0	12.0
Maximum	1,721.0	584.0	270.0	41,901.0	17,302.0	9,352.0	830.0	446.0	690.0
Minimum	−2.3	0.0	25.4	12.2	15.5	11.0	−3.3	1.0	3.0

SOURCES: IMF, EBRD, PlanEcon, World Bank.

Tables 3 and 4 both reveal that despite these shared shocks, the economic performance of the transition countries began to diverge within a few years of embarking on the change from planned to market economies. Growth rates spanned the spectrum from significant increases to large declines, and median inflation rates ranged from single digits to the high triple digits. The diversity of outcomes, combined with the comparable diversity of initial conditions and policy choices, naturally raises the question about the extent to which different starting points and choices have contributed to the differences in economic performance. A lively recent literature—including works by Aslund, Boone, and Johnson (1996), de Melo, Denizer, and Gelb (1996), Fischer, Sahay, and Vegh (1996a, 1996b, 1997), Sachs and Warner (1996), Selowsky and Martin (1997), and Berg et al. (1997)—examines the link between policy choices and outcomes. The emerging conclusion of these studies posits a quite sturdy positive correlation between progress toward the establishment of a market economy and better macroeconomic performance (faster growth and lower inflation). With few exceptions, these studies focus on the achieved degree, rather than the speed of, liberalization and thus shed less light on the distinction between persistent gradual and radical reformers.

The finding of a positive correlation between liberalization and economic performance, if indeed robust, does not permit an inference of causality and, thus, an assessment of the relative merits of alternative transition strategies. Such an inference would only be valid if the choice of transition strategy is itself random, specifically, if it is independent of any variable that might also influence performance. This condition is unlikely to be met. The subgroup of transition economies suffering from ethnic tension escalating into internal or external armed conflict, for example, retained tight central control over resources while substantially underperforming their peers as production plunged and reliance on money printing to finance military expenditures boosted inflation rates.

Viewed against their peer group, the experiences of these countries thus contribute to a negative link between liberalization and performance. A causal interpretation would be problematic, however, because the military conflict is arguably a primary cause of both the choice of transition strategy and the relative economic underperformance.

On the other end of the spectrum, the location of the Central European economies implied a possibility of future EU membership conditional on economic performance and adoption of a policy framework closely following the EU model, arguably influencing the cost-benefit calculus underlying the choice of transition strategy. At the same time, proximity, through gravity effects, yielded additional benefits to liberalization through enhanced trade and foreign-direct-investment (FDI) links with EU members. The experience of these countries, as compared to their peers, again contributes to a positive link between liberalization and performance. Once again, however, a third factor, in this case, location, arguably influenced both the choice of reform and the effects of reform, thus preventing simple causal inferences from strategy choice to outcome.

The *ex post* relative performance across observed strategies is thus insufficient to allow conclusions to be drawn about the *ex ante* hypothetical performance of a given transition economy under alternative strategies. To draw such conclusions, the dependence of the strategy choice on factors also influencing outcomes must explicitly be taken into account. Although space constraints prevent a full exploration of the issue here, Table 5 provides a casual window on these linkages, reporting the medians across the three transition strategies for five variables that the literature suggests have contributed to strategy choice (see de Melo et al., 1997, and Wolf, 1999, for in-depth assessments of some of these linkages). These five variables are (1) the initial industry share, proxying for the obsolescence shock, (2) the reported growth rates of net material product (NMP) during the late 1980s and the inflation rate in 1989 proxying for the inherited degree of economic instability,[1] (3) the distance from Vienna and from the nearest market economy, proxying for potential association effects arising from proximity to the EU and, thus, gravity effects on trade and FDI flows, (4) the starting

[1] Both of these series presumably suffer from severe mismeasurement. The premium of black market to official prices provides a more attractive measure of disequilibrium. However, the premium is not available for many of the sample economies. The same applies for a second alternative measure, real wage growth at official prices minus real consumption-good output growth.

TABLE 5

STRATEGY CHOICES AND INITIAL CONDITIONS: MEDIANS

	Radical	Gradual	Lagging
Initial industry share	45.0	44.0	43.0
1980s NMP growth	1.8	1.9	2.8
1989 inflation	0.6	1.5	0.6
Distance to nearest market economy (km)	251	362	1,021
Start of central planning (year)	1948	1945	1920

year of central planning, proxying for "memory effects" of operating under market conditions, and (5) the population share of the largest ethnic group, proxying for potential ethnic conflict.[2]

It is perhaps surprising that the initial degree of macroeconomic instability does not appear to be associated with the choice of strategy. Countries experiencing instability during the last years of central planning are no more likely to adopt radical or gradual reform than are countries entering the transition with a (relatively) stable macroeconomy. The size of the industrial sector, moreover, does not differ significantly across the three broad strategy types. The distance to the nearest market economy, by contrast, differs dramatically across the three strategies, ranging from 251 kilometers for the radical reformers to 1,021 for the laggards. Countries located close to market economies have adopted radical and gradual reforms far more frequently than have countries located far from market economies. Time spent under central planning also differs across strategies. Countries that did not adopt central planning until after World War II have tended to opt for gradual and radical reforms, whereas many that adopted central planning in the interwar period, including many of the non-Baltic successor states of the FSU, have lagged in the transition.

A detailed exploration of these links is beyond the scope of this study; its main concern is simply to note the existence of initial conditions that differ significantly across strategies and that might reasonably be expected also to influence outcomes. Distance to market economies and memory of markets, proxied by time under central planning, fulfill these conditions. These two variables are therefore used as controls in the discussion that follows.

[2] Although the list is not exclusive, a classification tree analysis reveals distance and time under central planning to be the dominant determinants of strategy choice, with the other variables playing secondary roles (Wolf, 1999).

5 CHOICES AND OUTCOMES OF TRANSITION STRATEGIES

Although the primary liberalization measure is continuous, it is instructive to begin exploring the link between reform choices and outcomes by returning to the discrete grouping of transition economies into radical, gradual, and lagging reformers described above. Table 6 reports the median value for all observations within a group for a range of performance indicators, using the unscaled growth rates.

TABLE 6

MEDIAN PERFORMANCE ACROSS REFORM STRATEGIES

	Radical	Gradual	Lagging
Real GDP growth	-0.9	-3.6	-8.9
Industrial-production growth	-3.7	-6.6	-7.8
Investment/GDP	20.0	26.6	25.7
Export growth	19.0	-4.5	0.1
GDP deflator	30.5	57.9	173.9
CPI inflation	32.1	84.8	219.4
Broad money growth	28.3	28.3	115.5
Velocity growth	1.3	5.8	49.5

In line with previous findings in the literature, the table suggests that radical reformers have outgrown the gradual reformers, which in turn have outgrown the lagging reformers. The higher growth rate is not associated with higher investment ratios, however, a finding that is in sharp contrast to one of the strongest stylized facts in the empirical growth literature. This fact suggests that better initial growth performance in transition economies depends not so much on the quantity of new investment as on changes in the efficiency of capital and labor use.[1] Export growth is much stronger for the radical reformers than for either the gradual or the lagging reformers, reflecting the strong surge in exports from Eastern Europe to the EU, albeit from very low levels.

[1] This "soft" growth coming from the reallocation of resources is, of course, temporary. In the long term, the traditional positive correlation between investment volume and growth is likely to emerge.

On the nominal side, radical reformers experienced substantially lower inflation than gradual reformers, both in terms of GDP deflators and CPI inflation rates. Gradual reformers, in turn, experienced lower inflation than lagging reformers. The ranking of inflation rates is matched by the ranking of monetary growth rates. Interestingly, however, differences in the growth rate of money and income do not fully account for the inflation differential: gradual and, in particular, lagging reformers also experienced a much faster velocity growth.

The evolution of output in the transition economies reflects the complex interaction of exogenous factors, such as the collapse of the Council for Mutual Economic Assistance, initial conditions, such as years under central planning, and transition strategy, which in turn depended partly on initial conditions. Table 7 presents a set of regressions to examine these links. The regressions are based on 125 observations and include a dummy for countries suffering internal or external military conflict (War) as well as a dummy for successor states of the FSU.

TABLE 7

REGRESSION RESULTS FOR GDP GROWTH

	(1) OLS	(2) OLS	(3) TSLS
Constant	-0.065 (1.97[a])	44.331 (2.12[a])	31.802 (1.20)
War	-0.063 (3.35[b])	-0.044 (2.05[a])	-0.101 (3.14[b])
FSU	-0.042 (2.04[a])	-0.061 (2.13[a])	-0.051 (1.42)
Liberalization at t	-0.213 (2.67[b])	-0.086 (0.94)	-0.033 (0.25)
Liberalization at t - 1	0.152 (1.49)	0.093 (0.93)	0.044 (0.31)
Liberalization at t - 2	0.202 (2.94[b])	0.121 (1.75)	0.196 (2.03[a]
Years under central planning		-13.484 (2.12[a])	-9.704 (1.21)
Distance to market economy		0.007 (0.26)	0.007 (0.21)
Fiscal deficit/GDP[c]		0.161 (1.96)	-0.343 (1.49)
Investment/GDP		-0.050 (0.60)	-0.232 (1.01)
Export growth		0.014 (1.15)	0.029 (0.64)
Exchange-rate regime[d]		-0.004 (0.19)	0.050 (1.11)
Inflation		-0.150 (3.15[b])	-0.096 (0.88)
Radical reformers		-0.011 (0.43)	-0.064 (1.70)
R^2	0.42	0.52	0.33
Adjusted R^2	0.40	0.47	0.25

NOTES: T-statistics are in parentheses.

[a] Denotes significance at the 5 percent level.

[b] Denotes significance at the 1 percent level.

[c] A fiscal deficit is coded as a negative number.

[d] Peg = 1; float = 2.

The first column relates the GDP growth rate to the current value and to two lags of the liberalization index. The lag structure attempts to capture the J-curve effect of creative destruction, at the cost of losing the 1989 and 1990 sample years (see Aslund, Boone, and Johnson, 1996; de Melo, Denizer, and Gelb, 1996; Fischer, Sahay, and Vegh, 1996a; and Berg et al., 1997). The coefficients on the liberalization measures capture three separate effects: first, the direct effect of liberalization on growth through, for example, improved factor allocation; second, the indirect effect of liberalization on growth through other growth determinants, for example, through a positive effect of liberalization on export growth; third, any effect of other excluded determinants of economic growth, including initial conditions, to the extent that the excluded variables are correlated with the indices. The coefficient pattern yields a J-curve effect. An increase in liberalization is associated with a negative impact on current growth, but with a positive lagged effect that cumulatively dominates the impact effect.

Differences in the liberalization indices account for 35 percent of the growth variance. Including the two dummies increases the multiple correlation coefficient (R^2) to 0.42. Although the exclusion of initial conditions and other growth determinants prohibits a causal interpretation of the coefficients, the relatively high joint explanatory power of the liberalization indices through the three channels identified is striking in itself. A simple regression of growth on the two initial conditions (years under central planning and distance from the nearest market economy) yields a substantially smaller R^2 of 0.128, suggesting that a dual dependence of growth outcomes and transition-strategy choice on initial conditions does not provide a full explanation of the observed correlation between liberalization and growth.

Column 2 of Table 7 reports a regression of growth on liberalization, the two initial conditions, a set of additional growth determinants (fiscal stance, investment share, export growth, exchange-rate regime, and inflation), and the dummy for radical reformers. The additional growth determinants potentially introduce a simultaneity bias in the regression. Column 3 reports the results of reestimating the equation with two-stage-least-squares (TSLS), using lagged values, the secondary enrollment rate, urbanization, and the initial share of industry as instruments.

Countries suffering armed conflict not surprisingly experience significantly lower growth, as do successor states of the FSU. Both variables are economically and, with one exception, statistically significant. Turning to the additional growth determinants, the fiscal stance does not exert a sturdy influence, perhaps partly because the measurement problems for this variable are particularly pronounced. Cross-country growth regressions typically find investment or savings ratios to be among the most important determinants of growth. As suggested by the medians reported above, this is not the case for the transition economies. The investment ratio comes in with a negative sign and is statistically insignificant. The failure to find an investment effect may reflect a distinction between quality and quantity. Because transition economies commenced from very high investment shares, investment quantities declined toward normal levels in the fastest liberalizing countries, which arguably also had the largest gains in investment efficiency.[2] Export growth enters the regressions positively but not significantly. Again, a distinction between quality and quantity may have been at work as reformers replaced trade within the bloc with more efficient trade with market economies, a feature not captured by aggregate trade growth.

Finally, inflation is associated with sharply lower growth, significantly so in the OLS but not the TSLS equation, a finding consistent with the view that stabilization is a necessary condition for a resumption of growth (Bruno, 1992, 1993; Bruno and Easterly, 1995; Fischer, Sahay, and Vegh, 1996a, 1996b).

Controlling for the additional growth determinants, the distance to the nearest market economy—associated with quite significant differences in strategy choice—plays no role and, indeed, is positive, although small and insignificant. The time spent under central planning enters negatively but, for the TSLS regression, insignificantly, suggesting that initial conditions do not exert an effect beyond an influence on the included growth determinants.

Turning to the liberalization indices, if liberalization in the first regression affected growth only through the added contemporaneous variables or was an indirect proxy for the initial conditions, the liberalization indices would become insignificant upon adding both sets of determinants. This is not the case. The J-curve found for the first regression is again present, and the group of indices remains significant, as does the two-year lagged index. This finding suggests the presence of additional, as yet unidentified, channels linking liberalization and growth. One obvious candidate for such a channel is the quality effect mentioned above. The residual effect of the liberalization index may pick up the positive growth effects of higher total factor productivity caused, in turn, by a more efficient allocation of resources not captured by the quantity measures.

[2] A direct regression of the investment ratio on the current and lagged liberalization indices yields a negative cumulative effect.

Although the results establish a positive link between the level of the liberalization index and growth, they do not by themselves establish a link between the speed of liberalization and growth, which is the crucial issue with regard to the relative merits of gradual versus radical transition strategies. The coefficient on the dummy for radical reformers picks up any effect of rapid reform conditional on controlling for the degree of liberalization attained. If speed matters, a significant positive coefficient would be expected. The dummy shows, however, a negative and insignificant effect, suggesting that what matters for a good growth performance is more the degree of liberalization than the speed with which it is attained, at least for the particular subjective definition of a radical strategy used here.

Like growth, inflation exhibits both shared and idiosyncratic elements across the transition economies. The majority of the transition countries started their journey from planned to market economies from a situation of latent excess demand, reflected in excess monetary balances. The overhang, combined with a highly distorted relative-price structure, triggered a period of inflation following the abandonment of quantity rationing as both absolute and relative prices adjusted. For the FSU republics, an additional inflationary impulse arose from the decision to maintain for a time a common ruble zone in the absence of effective mechanisms to constrain beggar-thy-neighbor monetary policies.

Despite the common shocks, cumulative inflation differs very significantly across the transition economies. These disparities again raise the question of whether the choice of transition strategy has played an important role in determining inflation outcomes.

Table 8, structured analogously to Table 7, provides some answers. The first column reports a regression of the inflation rate on the current liberalization index and two lags, as well as on the War and FSU dummies, yielding an inverted J-curve. More comprehensive liberalization is associated with a contemporaneous increase in inflation but with a decrease of inflation at both lags. A possible explanation for the positive contemporaneous effect is the downward adjustment of the excessive inherited real monetary balances, requiring a temporary excess of the inflation rate over the monetary growth rate. Including only the indices yields an R^2 of 0.396. Including the War and FSU dummies increases the explanatory power to 0.518. Differences in liberalization are thus able to account for a significant fraction of the differences in both growth and inflation performance in transition economies. Again, no causal interpretation is warranted, because the coefficient on the liberalization index captures a direct effect of liberalization on prices, an

TABLE 8

REGRESSION RESULTS FOR INFLATION

	(1) OLS	(2) OLS	(3) TSLS
Constant	0.551 (6.95[b])	-2.460 (0.07)	-40.860 (0.92)
War	0.161 (3.54[b])	0.144 (4.51)	0.183 (3.42[b])
FSU	0.210 (4.18[b])	0.093 (1.92)	0.139 (2.18[a])
Liberalization at t	0.139 (0.72)	0.218 (1.53)	0.366 (1.96)
Liberalization (t - 1)	-0.205 (0.83)	-0.237 (1.58)	-0.307 (1.60)
Liberalization (t - 2)	-0.328 (1.97[a])	-0.141 (1.36)	-0.129 (0.88)
Years under central planning		0.869 (0.08)	12.430 (0.92)
Distance to market economy		0.031 (0.70)	0.049 (0.94)
Fiscal deficit/GDP[c]		0.241 (1.97)	0.220 (0.835)
GDP growth		-0.364 (2.57[a])	-0.040 (0.07)
Broad money growth		0.478 (8.22[b])	0.805 (6.19[b])
Exchange-rate regime[d]		-0.175 (4.72[b])	-0.106 (1.70)
Exchange-rate-based stabiliza		0.105 (2.09[a])	0.123 (1.99[a])
Money-based stabilization		0.049 (1.50)	0.083 (1.77)
New currency		0.021 (0.65)	0.023 (0.61)
Radical reformers		-0.024 (0.54)	-0.022 (0.39)
R^2	0.518	0.847	0.800
Adjusted R^2	0.495	0.826	0.772

NOTES: T-statistics are in parentheses.

[a] Denotes significance at the 5 percent level.

[b] Denotes significance at the 1 percent level.

[c] A fiscal deficit is coded as a negative number.

[d] Peg = 1; float = 2.

indirect effect through other factors, and any chance correlation with other excluded variables.

Column 2 relates inflation to initial conditions, other potential determinants of inflation,[3] the liberalization index, and the dummy for radical reformers. To allow for simultaneity, column 3 reports the TSLS estimates, again using lags, the urbanization ratio, the initial share of industry, and the secondary enrollment ratio as instruments.

The results on the additional determinants are largely unsurprising. Higher GDP growth, a pegged exchange rate, and lower monetary

[3] These determinants include the fiscal deficit; GDP and broad money growth; dummies set equal to 1 if the country pursued an exchange-rate and money-based stabilization; the exchange-rate regime; and a dummy equal to 1 if the country adopted a new currency.

growth are associated with lower inflation.[4] Perhaps more unexpected, hybrid stabilizations are associated with inflation rates that are lower than those yielded by either pure exchange-rate or pure money-based stabilizations (Rebelo and Vegh, 1995; Sahay and Vegh, 1996; Fischer, Sahay, and Vegh, 1996a, 1996b). Controlling for these variables, a longer time spent under central planning and greater distance from a market economy are associated with higher inflation. The effects are insignificant, however, suggesting that any effects of initial conditions are captured by the liberalization index and the additional determinants.

If liberalization operates primarily through the additional determinants—notably by boosting GDP growth and reducing monetary growth—the coefficients on the liberalization indices should become insignificant once these determinants are added. As with the growth regression, this is not the case. The coefficients on the liberalization index exhibit the same inverted J-curve observed in the first regression and remain jointly significant, although the cumulative effect is sharply reduced. One plausible explanation for the residual negative effect of liberalization on inflation controlling for monetary and output growth is a positive credibility effect that restrains velocity growth in comprehensively liberalized economies (Anderson and Citrin, 1995). Finally, it is again interesting to ask whether the speed of liberalization exerts an independent influence beyond the negative link between the degree of liberalization and inflation. Although the coefficient on radical reformers is negative, it is quite small and economically insignificant.

[4] On the choice of exchange-rate regime and stabilization strategy, see Bruno (1993) and Calvo and Vegh (1994); for particular reference to transition economies, see Borensztein and Masson (1993).

6 CONCLUSION

The collapse of socialism in Eastern Europe raised the new policy challenge of managing the transition from planned to market economies. A wide variety of transition strategies have been put forward, centering on two views. The first view advocates a radical dismantling of controls in order to "jump the chasm in one leap," the second, stressing the advisability of "feeling the stones before crossing the river," proposes a gradual strategy of piecemeal removal of restrictions while paying close attention to institution building and the buffering of the social consequences of transition. Actual policy choices have matched the diversity of views, creating a unique natural experiment.

The evidence presented in this study suggests a sturdy J-curve linking the degree of liberalization to economic growth, and an equally sturdy inverted J-curve relating liberalization to inflation. Both results are robust to controlling for initial conditions that might influence both the strategy choice and outcomes, as well as to the inclusion of a standard set of determinants of growth and inflation. The latter finding is consistent with important quality effects of liberalization on growth as well as important credibility effects of liberalization on inflation, neither of which are well captured by the standard set of determinants.

Liberalization is thus robustly associated with a contemporaneous worsening of economic performance, but with significant gains in performance at the one- and two-year lags. These gains, furthermore, dominate the initial loss. Over a three-year period, an increase in liberalization has a positive cumulative effect on output and a negative cumulative effect on inflation. Controlling for the extent of liberalization attained, the speed with which the country has liberalized does not exert a significant independent effect on either growth or inflation. This leaves only a difficult-to-test dependency of the probability of attaining a specified level of liberalization on the speed of liberalization as a potential discriminant between the effects of gradual as opposed to radical strategies.

REFERENCES

Aghion, Phillipe, and Olivier Blanchard, "On the Speed of Adjustment in Central Europe," *NBER Macroeconomics Annual*, 1994, pp. 284–320.

Amsden, Alice, Jacek Kochanowicz, and Lance Taylor, *The Market Meets Its Match*, Cambridge, Mass., Harvard University Press, 1994.

Anderson, Jonathan, and Daniel Citrin, "The Behavior of Inflation and Velocity," in Daniel Citrin and Ashok Lahiri, eds., *Policy Experiences and Issues in the Baltics, Russia and Other Countries of the Former Soviet Union*, Occasional Paper No. 1333, Washington, D.C., International Monetary Fund, December 1995.

Aslund, Anders, "Lessons of the First Four Years of Systemic Change in Eastern Europe," *Journal of Comparative Economics*, 19 (August 1994), pp. 22–39.

Aslund, Anders, Peter Boone, and Simon Johnson, "How To Stabilize," *Brookings Papers on Economic Activity*, No. 1 (1996), pp. 217–313.

Atkinson, Anthony, and John Micklewright, *Economic Transformation in Eastern Europe and the Distribution of Income*, Cambridge and New York, Cambridge University Press, 1992.

Balcerowicz, Leszek, "Lessons and Consequences of the Left's Victory in Poland: Interview," *Transition Newsletter* (World Bank), 4 (October/November 1993), pp. 1–3.

———, "Common Fallacies in the Debate on the Economic Transition in Central and Eastern Europe," in Balcerowicz, *Socialism, Capitalism, Transformation*, New York, Central European University Press, 1995, pp. 232–269.

———, "The Interplay between Economic and Political Transition," in Salvatore Zecchini, ed., *Lessons from the Economic Transition*, 1997, pp. 153–168.

Balcerowicz, Leszek, and Alan Gelb, "Macropolicies in Transition to a Market Economy," in *Proceedings of the World Bank Annual Conference on Development Economics*, Washington, D.C., World Bank, 1994, pp. 21–56.

Berg, Andrew, Eduardo Borensztein, Ratna Sahay, and Jeromin Zettelmeyer, "The Evolution of Output in Transition Economies: How Different Is the FSU?" Washington, D.C., International Monetary Fund, Research Department, March 1997, processed.

Berg, Andrew, and Jeffrey Sachs, "Structural Adjustment and International Trade in Eastern Europe," *Economic Policy*, 14 (April 1992), pp. 117–173.

Blanchard, Olivier, Kenneth Froot, and Jeffrey Sachs, *Transition in Eastern Europe*, Chicago, Chicago University Press for National Bureau of Economic Research, 1994.

Bloem, Adriaan, Paul Cotterell, and Terry Gigantes, "National Accounts in Transition Countries: Distortions and Biases," International Monetary Fund Working Paper No. 96/130, Washington, D.C., International Monetary Fund, November 1996.

Borensztein, Eduardo, and Paul Masson, *Exchange Arrangements of Previously Centrally Planned Economies*, Occasional Paper No. 102, Washington, D.C., International Monetary Fund, February 1993.

Bruno, Michael, "Stabilization and Reform in Eastern Europe: A Preliminary Evaluation," *International Monetary Fund Staff Papers*, 39 (December 1992), pp. 741–777.

———, "Stabilization and the Macroeconomics of Transition—How Different is Eastern Europe?" *Economics of Transition*, 1 (January 1993), pp. 5–19.

Bruno, Michael, and William Easterly, "Inflation Crisis and Long-Run Growth," National Bureau of Economic Research Working Paper No. 5209, Cambridge, Mass., National Bureau of Economic Research, August 1995.

Calvo, Guillermo, and Carlos Vegh, "Inflation Stabilization and Nominal Anchors," *Contemporary Economic Policy*, 12 (April 1994), pp. 35–45.

de Melo, Martha, Cevdet Denizer, and Alan Gelb, "Patterns of Transition from Plan to Market," *World Bank Economic Review*, 10 (September 1996), pp. 397–424.

de Melo, Martha, Cevdet Denizer, Alan Gelb, and Stoyan Tenev, "Explaining Transition: The Role of Initial Conditions in Reforming Socialist Countries," Washington, D.C., World Bank, Policy Research Department, October 1997, processed.

Dewatripont, Mathias, and Gerard Roland, "The Virtues of Gradualism and Legitimacy in the Transition to a Market Economy," *Economic Journal*, 102 (March 1992), pp. 291–300.

Dornbusch, Rudiger, and Holger Wolf, "Curing a Monetary Overhang: Historical Lessons," forthcoming in Maurice Obstfeld, ed., *Festschrift for Robert Mundell*, Cambridge, Mass., MIT Press, 1999.

European Bank for Reconstruction and Development (EBRD), *Transition Report*, London, European Bank for Reconstruction and Development, 1994 and 1995.

Fischer, Stanley, Ratna Sahay, and Carlos Vegh, "Stabilization and Growth in Transition Economies: The Early Experience," *Journal of Economic Perspectives*, 10 (Spring 1996a), pp. 45–66.

———, "Economies in Transition: The Beginnings of Growth," *American Economic Review*, 86 (May 1996b), pp. 229–233.

———, "From Transition to Market: Evidence and Growth Prospects," in Salvatore Zecchini, ed., *Lessons from the Economic Transition*, 1997, pp. 79–102.

Ghosh, Atish, Anne-Marie Gulde, Jonathan Ostry, and Holger Wolf, "Does the Exchange Rate Regime Matter for Inflation and Growth?" *Economic Issues*,

No. 2, Washington, D.C., International Monetary Fund, September 1996.

Klaus, Vaclav, "Quotation of the Month: 'We Need an Untainted Market Economy, and We Need It Now'—Interview," *Transition Newsletter* (World Bank), 2 (September 1991), pp. 8–9.

———, "The Ten Commandments Revisited," *International Economy*, 7 (September/October 1993), pp. 36–39 and 70.

Koen, Vincent, "Measuring the Transition: A User's View on National Accounts in Russia," International Monetary Fund Working Paper No. 94/6, Washington, D.C., International Monetary Fund, January 1994.

Kornai, Janos, *The Socialist System: The Political Economy of Communism*, Princeton, N.J., Princeton University Press, 1992.

———, "Transformational Recession: The Main Causes," *Journal of Comparative Economics*, 19 (August 1994), pp. 39–63.

Laban, Raul, and Holger Wolf, "Large Scale Privatization in Transition Economies," *American Economic Review*, 83 (December 1993), pp. 1199–1210.

Lipton, David, and Jeffrey Sachs, "Creating a Market Economy in Eastern Europe," *Brookings Papers on Economic Activity*, No. 1 (1990), pp. 75–133.

Murrell, Peter, "What Is Shock Therapy? What Did It Do in Poland and Russia?" *Post-Soviet Affairs*, 9 (April-June 1993), pp. 111–140.

———, "The Transition According to Cambridge, Mass," *Journal of Economic Literature*, 33 (March 1995), pp. 164–178.

———, "How Far Has the Transition Progressed?" *Journal of Economic Perspectives*, 10 (Spring 1996), pp. 25–44.

Rebelo, Sergio, and Carlos Vegh, "Real Effects of Exchange Rate Based Stabilization," *NBER Macroeconomics Annual* (1995), pp. 125–174.

Sachs, Jeffrey, *Poland's Jump to the Market Economy*, Cambridge, Mass., MIT Press, 1993.

———, "Reforms in Eastern Europe and the Former Soviet Union in Light of the East Asian Experiences," National Bureau of Economic Research Working Paper No. 5404, Cambridge, Mass., National Bureau of Economic Research, January 1996.

Sachs, Jeffrey, and Andrew Warner, "Achieving Rapid Growth in the Transition Economies of Central Europe," Development Discussion Paper No. 544, Cambridge, Mass., Harvard Institute for International Development, July 1996.

Sahay, Ratna, and Carlos Vegh, "Inflation and Stabilization in Transition Economies: An Analytical Interpretation of the Evidence," *Journal of Policy Reform*, 1 (No. 1, 1996), pp. 75–108.

Selowsky, Marek, and Ricardo Martin, "Policy Performance and Output Growth in the Transition Economies," *American Economic Review*, 87 (May 1997), pp. 349–353.

Siebert, Horst, Martin Raiser, and Rolf Langhammer, "The Transition in Central and Eastern Europe," Kiel, Institute of World Economics, 1996, processed.

Taylor, Lance, "The Market Met Its Match: Lessons for the Future from the Transition's Initial Years," *Journal of Comparative Economics*, 19 (August 1994), pp. 64–87.

Weitzman, Martin, "Economic Transition: Can Theory Help?" *European Economic Review*, 37 (April 1993), pp. 549–555.

Winiecki, Jan, "The Inevitability of a Fall in Output in the Early Stages of Transition to the Market: Theoretical Underpinnings," *Soviet Studies* (U.K.), 43 (No. 4, 1991), pp. 669–676.

Wolf, Holger, "Determinants of Policy Choices in Transition Economies," Washington, D.C., Georgetown University, Center for German and European Studies, May 1999, processed.

World Bank, *Historically Planned Economies*, Washington, D.C., 1993.

———, *World Development Report*, Washington, D.C., World Bank, 1996.

Zecchini, Salvatore, ed., *Lessons from the Economic Transition: Central and Eastern Europe in the 1990s*, Dordrecht, Boston, and London, Kluwer, 1997.

PUBLICATIONS OF THE
INTERNATIONAL FINANCE SECTION

Notice to Contributors

The International Finance Section publishes papers in four series: ESSAYS IN INTERNATIONAL FINANCE, PRINCETON STUDIES IN INTERNATIONAL FINANCE, and SPECIAL PAPERS IN INTERNATIONAL ECONOMICS contain new work not published elsewhere. REPRINTS IN INTERNATIONAL FINANCE reproduce journal articles previously published by Princeton faculty members associated with the Section. The Section welcomes the submission of manuscripts for publication under the following guidelines:

ESSAYS are meant to disseminate new views about international financial matters and should be accessible to well-informed nonspecialists as well as to professional economists. Technical terms, tables, and charts should be used sparingly; mathematics should be avoided.

STUDIES are devoted to new research on international finance, with preference given to empirical work. They should be comparable in originality and technical proficiency to papers published in leading economic journals. They should be of medium length, longer than a journal article but shorter than a book.

SPECIAL PAPERS are surveys of research on particular topics and should be suitable for use in undergraduate courses. They may be concerned with international trade as well as international finance. They should also be of medium length.

Manuscripts should be submitted in triplicate, typed single sided and double spaced throughout on 8½ by 11 white bond paper. Publication can be expedited if manuscripts are computer keyboarded in WordPerfect or a compatible program. Additional instructions and a style guide are available from the Section.

How to Obtain Publications

The Section's publications are distributed free of charge to college, university, and public libraries and to nongovernmental, nonprofit research institutions. Eligible institutions may ask to be placed on the Section's permanent mailing list.

Individuals and institutions not qualifying for free distribution may receive all publications for the calendar year for a subscription fee of $40.00. Late subscribers will receive all back issues for the year during which they subscribe.

Publications may be ordered individually, with payment made in advance. ESSAYS and REPRINTS cost $9.00 each; STUDIES and SPECIAL PAPERS cost $12.50. An additional $1.50 should be sent for postage and handling within the United States, Canada, and Mexico; $1.75 should be added for surface delivery outside the region.

All payments must be made in U.S. dollars. Subscription fees and charges for single issues will be waived for organizations and individuals in countries where foreign-exchange regulations prohibit dollar payments.

Information about the Section and its publishing program is available at the Section's website at www.princeton.edu/~ifs. A subscription and order form is printed at the end of this volume. Correspondence should be addressed to:

International Finance Section
Department of Economics, Fisher Hall
Princeton University
Princeton, New Jersey 08544-1021
Tel: 609-258-4048 • Fax: 609-258-6419
E-mail: ifs@princeton.edu

List of Recent Publications

A complete list of publications is available at the International Finance Section website at www.princeton.edu/~ifs.

ESSAYS IN INTERNATIONAL FINANCE

176. Graham Bird, *Loan-Loss Provisions and Third-World Debt.* (November 1989)
177. Ronald Findlay, *The "Triangular Trade" and the Atlantic Economy of the Eighteenth Century: A Simple General-Equilibrium Model.* (March 1990)
178. Alberto Giovannini, *The Transition to European Monetary Union.* (November 1990)
179. Michael L. Mussa, *Exchange Rates in Theory and in Reality.* (December 1990)
180. Warren L. Coats, Jr., Reinhard W. Furstenberg, and Peter Isard, *The SDR System and the Issue of Resource Transfers.* (December 1990)
181. George S. Tavlas, *On the International Use of Currencies: The Case of the Deutsche Mark.* (March 1991)
182. Tommaso Padoa-Schioppa, ed., with Michael Emerson, Kumiharu Shigehara, and Richard Portes, *Europe After 1992: Three Essays.* (May 1991)
183. Michael Bruno, *High Inflation and the Nominal Anchors of an Open Economy.* (June 1991)
184. Jacques J. Polak, *The Changing Nature of IMF Conditionality.* (September 1991)
185. Ethan B. Kapstein, *Supervising International Banks: Origins and Implications of the Basle Accord.* (December 1991)
186. Alessandro Giustiniani, Francesco Papadia, and Daniela Porciani, *Growth and Catch-Up in Central and Eastern Europe: Macroeconomic Effects on Western Countries.* (April 1992)
187. Michele Fratianni, Jürgen von Hagen, and Christopher Waller, *The Maastricht Way to EMU.* (June 1992)
188. Pierre-Richard Agénor, *Parallel Currency Markets in Developing Countries: Theory, Evidence, and Policy Implications.* (November 1992)
189. Beatriz Armendariz de Aghion and John Williamson, *The G-7's Joint-and-Several Blunder.* (April 1993)
190. Paul Krugman, *What Do We Need to Know About the International Monetary System?* (July 1993)
191. Peter M. Garber and Michael G. Spencer, *The Dissolution of the Austro-Hungarian Empire: Lessons for Currency Reform.* (February 1994)
192. Raymond F. Mikesell, *The Bretton Woods Debates: A Memoir.* (March 1994)
193. Graham Bird, *Economic Assistance to Low-Income Countries: Should the Link be Resurrected?* (July 1994)
194. Lorenzo Bini-Smaghi, Tommaso Padoa-Schioppa, and Francesco Papadia, *The Transition to EMU in the Maastricht Treaty.* (November 1994)
195. Ariel Buira, *Reflections on the International Monetary System.* (January 1995)
196. Shinji Takagi, *From Recipient to Donor: Japan's Official Aid Flows, 1945 to 1990 and Beyond.* (March 1995)
197. Patrick Conway, *Currency Proliferation: The Monetary Legacy of the Soviet Union.* (June 1995)

198. Barry Eichengreen, *A More Perfect Union? The Logic of Economic Integration.* (June 1996)
199. Peter B. Kenen, ed., with John Arrowsmith, Paul De Grauwe, Charles A. E. Goodhart, Daniel Gros, Luigi Spaventa, and Niels Thygesen, *Making EMU Happen—Problems and Proposals: A Symposium.* (August 1996)
200. Peter B. Kenen, ed., with Lawrence H. Summers, William R. Cline, Barry Eichengreen, Richard Portes, Arminio Fraga, and Morris Goldstein, *From Halifax to Lyons: What Has Been Done about Crisis Management?* (October 1996)
201. Louis W. Pauly, *The League of Nations and the Foreshadowing of the International Monetary Fund.* (December 1996)
202. Harold James, *Monetary and Fiscal Unification in Nineteenth-Century Germany: What Can Kohl Learn from Bismarck?* (March 1997)
203. Andrew Crockett, *The Theory and Practice of Financial Stability.* (April 1997)
204. Benjamin J. Cohen, *The Financial Support Fund of the OECD: A Failed Initiative.* (June 1997)
205. Robert N. McCauley, *The Euro and the Dollar.* (November 1997)
206. Thomas Laubach and Adam S. Posen, *Disciplined Discretion: Monetary Targeting in Germany and Switzerland.* (December 1997)
207. Stanley Fischer, Richard N. Cooper, Rudiger Dornbusch, Peter M. Garber, Carlos Massad, Jacques J. Polak, Dani Rodrik, and Savak S. Tarapore, *Should the IMF Pursue Capital-Account Convertibility?* (May 1998)
208. Charles P. Kindleberger, *Economic and Financial Crises and Transformations in Sixteenth-Century Europe.* (June 1998)
209. Maurice Obstfeld, *EMU: Ready or Not?* (July 1998)
210. Wilfred Ethier, *The International Commercial System.* (September 1998)
211. John Williamson and Molly Mahar, *A Survey of Financial Liberalization.* (November 1998)
212. Ariel Buira, *An Alternative Approach to Financial Crises.* (February 1999)
213. Barry Eichengreen, Paul Masson, Miguel Savastano, and Sunil Sharma, *Transition Strategies and Nominal Anchors on the Road to Greater Exchange-Rate Flexibility.* (April 1999)
214. Curzio Giannini, *"Enemy of None but a Common Friend of All"? An International Perspective on the Lender-of-Last-Resort Function.* (June 1999)

PRINCETON STUDIES IN INTERNATIONAL FINANCE

66. Helmut Reisen, *Public Debt, External Competitiveness, and Fiscal Discipline in Developing Countries.* (November 1989)
67. Victor Argy, Warwick McKibbin, and Eric Siegloff, *Exchange-Rate Regimes for a Small Economy in a Multi-Country World.* (December 1989)
68. Mark Gersovitz and Christina H. Paxson, *The Economies of Africa and the Prices of Their Exports.* (October 1990)
69. Felipe Larraín and Andrés Velasco, *Can Swaps Solve the Debt Crisis? Lessons from the Chilean Experience.* (November 1990)
70. Kaushik Basu, *The International Debt Problem, Credit Rationing and Loan Pushing: Theory and Experience.* (October 1991)

71. Daniel Gros and Alfred Steinherr, *Economic Reform in the Soviet Union: Pas de Deux between Disintegration and Macroeconomic Destabilization.* (November 1991)
72. George M. von Furstenberg and Joseph P. Daniels, *Economic Summit Declarations, 1975-1989: Examining the Written Record of International Cooperation.* (February 1992)
73. Ishac Diwan and Dani Rodrik, *External Debt, Adjustment, and Burden Sharing: A Unified Framework.* (November 1992)
74. Barry Eichengreen, *Should the Maastricht Treaty Be Saved?* (December 1992)
75. Adam Klug, *The German Buybacks, 1932-1939: A Cure for Overhang?* (November 1993)
76. Tamim Bayoumi and Barry Eichengreen, *One Money or Many? Analyzing the Prospects for Monetary Unification in Various Parts of the World.* (September 1994)
77. Edward E. Leamer, *The Heckscher-Ohlin Model in Theory and Practice.* (February 1995)
78. Thorvaldur Gylfason, *The Macroeconomics of European Agriculture.* (May 1995)
79. Angus S. Deaton and Ronald I. Miller, *International Commodity Prices, Macroeconomic Performance, and Politics in Sub-Saharan Africa.* (December 1995)
80. Chander Kant, *Foreign Direct Investment and Capital Flight.* (April 1996)
81. Gian Maria Milesi-Ferretti and Assaf Razin, *Current-Account Sustainability.* (October 1996)
82. Pierre-Richard Agénor, *Capital-Market Imperfections and the Macroeconomic Dynamics of Small Indebted Economies.* (June 1997)
83. Michael Bowe and James W. Dean, *Has the Market Solved the Sovereign-Debt Crisis?* (August 1997)
84. Willem H. Buiter, Giancarlo M. Corsetti, and Paolo A. Pesenti, *Interpreting the ERM Crisis: Country-Specific and Systemic Issues* (March 1998)
85. Holger C. Wolf, *Transition Strategies: Choices and Outcomes* (June 1999)

SPECIAL PAPERS IN INTERNATIONAL ECONOMICS

16. Elhanan Helpman, *Monopolistic Competition in Trade Theory.* (June 1990)
17. Richard Pomfret, *International Trade Policy with Imperfect Competition.* (August 1992)
18. Hali J. Edison, *The Effectiveness of Central-Bank Intervention: A Survey of the Literature After 1982.* (July 1993)
19. Sylvester W.C. Eijffinger and Jakob De Haan, *The Political Economy of Central-Bank Independence.* (May 1996)

REPRINTS IN INTERNATIONAL FINANCE

28. Peter B. Kenen, *Ways to Reform Exchange-Rate Arrangements*; reprinted from *Bretton Woods: Looking to the Future*, 1994. (November 1994)
29. Peter B. Kenen, *Sorting Out Some EMU Issues*; reprinted from Jean Monnet Chair Paper 38, Robert Schuman Centre, European University Institute, 1996. (December 1996)

fold over, seal, and send

◦ SUBSCRIBE ◦ ORDER ◦

INTERNATIONAL FINANCE SECTION

SUBSCRIPTIONS

Rate $40 a year

The International Finance Section issues six to eight publications each year in a mix of Essays, Studies, and occasional Special Papers and Reprints. Late subscribers receive all publications for the subscription year. Prepayment is required and may be made by check in U.S. dollars or by Visa or MasterCard. A complete list of publications is available at www.princeton.edu/~ifs.

Address inquiries to:

International Finance Section
Department of Economics, Fisher Hall
Princeton University
Princeton, NJ 08544–1021

BOOK ORDERS

Essays & Reprints	$9.00
Studies & Special Papers	$12.50

plus postage

Within U.S.	$1.50
Outside U.S. (surface mail)	$1.75

Discounts are available for book dealers and for orders of five or more publications.

Telephone: 609–258–4048
Telefax: 609–258–6419
E-mail: ifs@princeton.edu

fold up

INTERNATIONAL FINANCE SECTION

This is a subscription ☐ ; a book order ☐

Essay #(s) _____, _____ No. of copies___

Study #(s) _____, _____ No. of copies___

Special Paper # _____ No. of copies___

Reprint # _____ No. of copies___

☐ Enclosed is my check made payable to Princeton University, International Finance Section

totaling $______________.

Please charge: ☐ Visa ☐ MasterCard

Acct.# ________________________________

Expires ________________________________

Signature________________________________

Send to:

Name________________________________

Address________________________________

City________________________________

State __________________Zip __________

Country________________________________

FIRST
CLASS
POSTAGE
HERE

INTERNATIONAL FINANCE SECTION
DEPARTMENT OF ECONOMICS
FISHER HALL
PRINCETON UNIVERSITY
PRINCETON, NJ 08544-1021